WEIGHT LOSS HYPNOSIS FOR BUSY MOMS

The Complete Lose Weight Guide with Hypnosis and Guided Meditation for Busy Moms Who Only Have a Few Minutes a Day

EMILY BAILEY – HYPNOSIS ACADEMY

Table of Contents

Chapter 1.

Why Hypnosis?

Now that we understand how our mind works, let us start talking about hypnosis. Hypnosis is a relaxation technique, in which we follow the steps to achieve a state of higher concentration and relaxation. This is called a "hypnotic state" and is similar to daydreaming or the feeling of losing track of time after driving for long periods (called "road hypnosis").

Under hypnosis, we are still very much in control. In the hypnotic state, you are only relaxed and highly focused. This allows you to achieve a high state of consciousness. In the hypnotic state, the mind is highly suggestible. That is why hypnosis is so powerful.

Most bad habits, negative inclinations, and phobias are all triggered by our unconscious thoughts. A smoker tends to have automatic cravings, which triggers the conscious mind to reach for a cigarette. But under hypnosis, the smoker can reformulate these unconscious impulses. First, he/she must figure out the triggers of these automatic thoughts to begin with. Then, start removing and replacing them with more positive associations.

In other words, positive thoughts are pushed to the front of the unconscious and stifle the old way of thinking. This is why hypnosis works. It gets you to the root cause of your habit or fixation. Well, this is a very broad overview of what hypnosis is.

You probably have some unanswered questions. I will help you investigate hypnosis on a deeper level, including providing information on what hypnosis is, what actually happens in the brain during hypnosis and what you can do to get started.

Understand What Hypnosis Is

Hypnosis is sometimes referred to as the hypnotic state. This is the relaxed and highly focused mental structure that you achieve after being hypnotized.

You can come to think of hypnosis as meditation with a goal. Both are similar in the sense that they will try to achieve a state of relaxation and concentration. But with hypnosis, you go one step further. In this state of intense awareness, you begin to examine your subconscious and receive suggestions that can help you reformulate and improve the functioning of the subconscious. The process generally includes three steps:

Phase #1: Hypnotic induction

The hypnotic induction is the first phase you must follow to achieve hypnosis. Usually, you will be sitting in a chair, lying on a bed, or anywhere comfortable with your eyes closed. You can also use a script and/or controlled breathing techniques to relax your mind and focus.

Phase #2: Hypnotic state

Now the hypnotic state is reached. In the hypnotic state, you feel physically and mentally relaxed; you are so calm and focused on heightened awareness.

Phase #3: Hypnotic suggestions

Once in hypnosis, your mind becomes highly suggestible. In this phase, your mind receives hypnotic suggestions. These suggestions are meant to replace and update old ways in your subconscious thoughts.

How Does Hypnosis Work?

I just showed you a breakdown of the phases of hypnosis. But how does hypnosis work? In hypnosis, we can reformulate our unconscious thoughts. You may wonder: why is the hypnotized mind so suggestible? What happens in the brain when we are hypnotized? Can everyone be hypnotized? The short answer is we can likely all be hypnotized!

According to research, the majority of people, about 75-85 percent, can achieve a slight trance. And most of these people share some common traits such as:

- Daydream often.
- Get absorbed in daily activities quickly.
- Show more empathy.
- Are open-minded about hypnosis.

Of course, it is not necessary to show all or one of these to be hypnotized. But they offer more susceptibility to hypnosis. However, even for those who do not achieve a mild hypnotic state, there are still benefits to hypnosis.

What Happens to the Brain?

There are a lot of theories as to why hypnosis work. However, the relevant thought here is that hypnosis helps us achieve a state of deep concentration and relaxation, which allows us to avoid the conscious mind.

Recent research confirms part of this theory. One study showed that the areas of the brain responsible for critical thinking show reduced activity under hypnosis. Other studies on brain activity during hypnosis confirms that hypnosis allowed us to:

- Stimulates stimuli: This describes a reduced activity in the anterior dorsal cingulate of the brain. This part forms our awareness network. That is, under hypnosis, we can adjust our worries and stress. And we get absorbed in the experience.

- Increased mind-brain connections: studies show that the mind is more in tune with how it controls the body. This explains how hypnotic suggestions help us manage how our body responds to specific situations, such as overcoming fears, cravings, or negative responses.
- Reduced self-consciousness: Studies show the connection between two brain networks. This explains why we become much less aware of our actions, and therefore more suggestible.

Overall, this shows that our brains behave differently in the hypnotic state. In fact, many of these processes are unique to hypnosis.

What Does the Hypnotic State Feel Like?

You may be wondering, "What exactly do I feel in the hypnotic state?" You could describe your feelings as being in deep relaxation or the trance state. You will feel hyper receptive but relaxed, as you would feel during meditation.

When entering hypnosis, you may feel some physical sensations such as relaxation and heaviness around your muscles, such as the eyelids. You can feel your body. You will bypass your conscious mind, enter your subconscious mind, and push out negative associations. Most people describe the hypnotic state as a feeling of having a nap. However, the difference is during hypnosis, you are conscious and guided through an experience.

What Can Be Achieved with Hypnosis?

Your subconscious mind controls almost all of your thinking. About 95 percent of your thoughts are independently generated through the unconscious mind. This is why we get caught doing unwanted behaviors. They are deeply embedded in our minds due to repetition and reinforcement. Many of our fears, worries, habits, impulses and doubts. Therefore, remain unconscious.

Under hypnosis, we try to reformulate and reverse these "thought patterns." Therefore, hypnotherapy has been shown to be very useful for unconsciously motivating habits.

The Betty Erickson Method

Betty Erickson developed this hypnosis technique. Although Betty was not a hypnotist, she understood how our visual-auditory-kinesthetic systems influenced our world in a trance state. This technique has become increasingly popular in the world of hypnosis. This hypnosis technique can be used to relieve stress or any other self-hypnosis you would like to do.

The basic principles:

They Are All Thoughts in the Form of Images, Full of Sounds and Emotions

When we visualize, we think of all possible scenarios. We imagine how it is now, how we want it to be, and what it will be like in the future. This is simply a mixture of images that are already stored in the brain.

In the same way, our thoughts are associated with sounds, which are also the result of information stored in our minds, such as songs and sounds we imagine, speaking or hearing. These sounds also include background noises and sounds we make when in dialogue with ourselves and others.

Emotions are the third way we think. These could be what we have experienced before or what we want to try or experience. Although our conscious mind uses these three, more often, only one is dominant. Therefore, for someone who associates his thoughts with sounds, he will not be as successful if he mainly uses visuals.

Before you move on to self-hypnosis, you may want to set goals for what you want to happen. Once you are ready, follow these steps.

Step 1: **Get Comfortable**

Sit or lie down in a quiet and comfortable position.

Relax your mind and body and feel yourself begin to wander in a state of relaxation. Let yourself in for a bit while staying on top of the outside world and keeping your eyes open, but you start to sleep.

Step 2: **Focus on Something You Are Seeing**

Shadows moving across the wall or unique surroundings motifs can provide something unique to see. Be aware of what you see and become aware of it. Do it three different times, with three different objects.

Step 3: **Focus on Something You Are Listening to**

This could be the sound of your breathing, the wind brushing against the windows, or the hum of the air conditioner. Find three different things and observe them and bring them to your knowledge.

Step 4: **Focus on Something You Feel**

Maybe it is the movement of muscles along the joints, the gap between the shoulder blades, the weight of the feet on the floor, or the weight of the body on the chair. Consider three things and become aware of them.

Step 5: **Continue With Two Things, Then One Thing**

Repeat steps 2-4, and this time, you will see two things, hear two things, and feel two things. So, do the same for one thing.

Step 6: **Close Your Eyes and Go Inward**

Allow yourself to go inward and relax and feel slightly drifting. This is a calm and peaceful state where you can simply let it go.

Step 7: **Imagine a New or Old Show**

This could be what you saw before, or it could be something completely new. Imagine something you can see. Maybe it is a purple elephant, maybe it is a soothing blue light, or perhaps it is the sight of a ship taking off.

Step 8: **Imagine an Old or New Sound**

You can create a sound, or it can be something you are already familiar with. An example is that you can hear the sound of an animal in nature, or a spacecraft suspended in space or the relaxing rain that falls on a group of leaves.

Step 9: **Imagine an Old or New Feeling**

Become aware of something you have noticed before, or perhaps something you want to pay more attention to, such as how your breathing feels when it enters your lungs and the relaxation around your clavicle when you exhale.

Step 10: **Now, You Are in Hypnosis!**

In this hypnotic state, you can make suggestions or just relax and let the ideas take effect that you had in mind before starting the session. The only trust that your mind is letting suggestions circulate: the more you can get carried away, the easier your ideas will take root inside.

Step 11: **Emerge**

Say to yourself, "As I count from 1 to 5, I shall emerge with a great sense of energy, feeling refreshed and relaxed."

So, count from 1 to 5, allowing as much time as your body needs to make it real for you.

Chapter 2.

Self-Hypnotic Suggestions

HOW EFFECTIVE IS HYPNOSIS?

Self-hypnosis undertaken for self-improvement has become increasingly popular for numerous people. The number of hypnosis techniques and self-hypnosis methods for making the mind go into a trance, and self-hypnosis instruction or guides are getting more and more popular. However, the best way of learning how to get effective self-hypnosis is learning directly from a qualified and experienced hypnotherapist.

Essentially, self-hypnosis is learned for positive self-change irrespective of the level and can work from light trance to deep hypnosis. Hypnosis for positive change is all about getting into a different frame of mind to increase your options and find new ways to solve problems. Self-hypnosis can only be limited by imagination.

Methods of Self-Hypnosis

The process of facilitating the direction of your hypnosis is simple: choose your intention and, when you are ready and have entered the hypnotic state, begin repeating your intention to direct your awareness and influence your subconscious. However, you may find that it is harder to enter a state of hypnosis when you do not have someone directly telling you what to do when to do it, or how long to do it for. For that reason, you may be curious about how you can enter a state of hypnosis on your own so that you can even begin to facilitate change in the first place.

We will explore different practices you can use to enter a deep hypnotic trance on your own and begin practicing self-hypnosis right away. These different practices are unique in their own right, and each one can help you enter a deep trance-like state so that self-hypnosis is possible.

We will explore such a wide range of options because many people find that certain practices do not work as well for them as others do. For that reason, you may be interested in playing around with a variety of different techniques so that you can learn which ones will work best for you. You may find that as you become particularly experienced with one, it becomes even more useful for you as you can use it and enter a state of hypnosis far quicker. However, you may also find that using one too frequently can result in you expecting hypnosis and therefore actually struggling to enter a deep trance-like state. If you find the latter is true, then you may consider trying a new practice from the list so that you can rediscover your hypnotic trance and gain maximum results from your self-hypnosis practice. This practice is personal to you, so do not be afraid to do whatever it is that you need to so you can maximize your success in entering your trance-like state and experiencing success in your self-hypnosis practice.

To get positive change, an individual should:

1. Create a goal and capture it in writing. The self-hypnosis goal should be concise and precise. By writing down your statement of intent you solidify the idea of what you want in your mind and give your subconscious mind something to work towards.

2. The goal must be personal, positive, achievable, and put in the present tense. Create a written statement that only includes the things you want to have and it must not concentrate, in any way, on the things you no longer wish to experience.

Examples of using the positive statements would be "I achieve my ideal weight with ease" rather than "I am no longer overweight." The mind works with images and when you focus on not being overweight your mind creates a picture of being overweight.

For example, you might want hypnosis for self-improvement and having high self-esteem. The goal can be:

'I am happy that I can always hold my head high and feel contented.'

An individual can always play around with the words used to state the goal to make sure that the statement truly means something for you. By following this advice, you ensure that the only picture your mind forms are positive. During self-hypnosis, when you recall these pictures, you are instructing your subconscious mind to help you create them.

For practice, read the statement you have created and started becoming aware of the pictures you are seeing in your mind. Make these pictures larger, brighter, and more emotional. Alter the mental scene until it becomes exactly as you would want it to be in reality. Imagine the words are true, feel how it would feel if those words were true right now, right here. Keep changing it until it makes you feel really great. The written statement and mental pictures combined with positive emotions are the blueprints for success during self-hypnosis.

People tend to have some very strange ideas about hypnosis. They think about a man standing in front of them, you're getting sleepy, very sleepy, and they even worry about doing things they would not normally do when they under hypnosis. For that reason, I want to take some time to explain what hypnosis is.

To put it simply, hypnosis is an altered state of consciousness that opens you up to suggestions. This means that while you are under hypnosis you are more likely to accept suggestions because your subconscious is bypassed so it is not able to ask the 'what-if' questions.

The suggestion is accepted by the subconscious, therefore, suggesting reality. Think about it like this. You can be hypnotized and told that you cannot speak. This will automatically become your reality and you will not be able to speak.

In the same way that hypnosis can be used to make you not be able to speak, it can also unlock the potential within yourself that will allow you to accomplish many things.

You see, many of us fail or even fail to try because our conscious mind does not believe in what we want to be true. For example, if a person wants to try a specific career, they will tell themselves that they are not smart enough for that career or they will not succeed.

If you can bypass these thoughts by using hypnosis, making success a reality in your life you will be able to do anything you want in life.

It is important to remember that when you are using hypnosis, it does not matter if the suggestion originates with you during self-hypnosis or if it originates with a person who is hypnotizing you.

You should also know that when you are hypnotized by another person or a recording, that person can't make you do something you don't really want to do. It is also impossible for you to be hypnotized if you do not want to be. This means you don't have to worry about someone hypnotizing you or making you do things that you don't want to do.

When you undergo hypnosis, you need to make sure you are completely relaxed and not distracted. If you are not relaxed or there are distractions you will not be fully hypnotized therefore you will not receive all of the benefits of hypnosis.

What Are Some of the Benefits of Hypnosis?

There are some great benefits of hypnosis, most of the time it depends on what the hypnosis is focusing on. For example, you can focus on positive living, and hypnosis can help remove negative thoughts. You can focus on quitting smoking or losing weight and the hypnosis will make these processes much easier than if you were trying to do it on your own.

Hypnosis can help with concentration, productivity, and even help with keeping a clear mind. Many people who are suffering from mental disorders have also found that hypnosis helps them stop taking medication.

All of us can benefit from hypnosis in our lives and it is up to us to decide how to use hypnosis to best benefit us. If you are going to use hypnosis you need to make sure you are going to stick with it and use it every day. It will not benefit you if you only remember to use hypnosis once a week or only think about it when things get especially hard in your life. You need to make time each day, at least 30 minutes and I suggest doing this twice a day if you want to see the best results.

The name is unlocking your magical powers with hypnosis but I am going to tell you right now you are not going to be disappearing and reappearing somewhere else, you are not going to levitate or do any other so-called magical trick. These powers that I am going to teach you are going to be powers of the mind as well as the body.

For example, you can unlock psychic powers with meditation, you can unlock healing powers as well which we will go over. I don't want you to feel as if you are going to learn 'magic' when in reality you are going to unlock natural powers.

You see, these natural powers have always been there and everyone possesses them but since we only use about 40 percent of our brains, we need help unlocking them.

Chapter 3.

Guided Meditation

Meditation Exercise 1: Release of Bad Habits

S it comfortably. Relax your muscles, close your eyes. Breathe in and breathe out. Do not cross your feet because this will lock you away from the desired experience. Hold your hands together to connect your logical brain hemisphere with your instinct.

Concentrate on your back now and notice how you feel in the bed or chair you are sitting in. Take a deep breath and let your stress leave your body. Now focus on your neck. Observe how your neck is joined to your shoulders. Lift your shoulders slowly. Breathe in slowly and release it. Feel how your shoulders loosen. Lift your shoulders again a little bit then let them relax. Observe how your neck muscles are tensing and how much pressure it has. Breathe in and breathe out slowly. Release the pressure in your neck and notice how the stress is leaving your body. Repeat the whole exercise from the beginning. Observe your back. Notice all the stress and let it go with a profound breath. Focus on your shoulders and neck again. Lift up your shoulders and hold it for some moments, then release your shoulders again and let all the stress go away. Sense how the stress is going away. Now, focus your attention to your back. Feel how comfortable it is. Focus on your whole body. While breathing in, let relaxation come, and while you are breathing out, let frustration leave your body. Notice how much you are relaxed.

Know that your soul is perfect as it is, and all you want is for everything that pulls away to leave. With every breath, let your old beliefs go, as you are creating more and more space for something new. After spending a few minutes with this, imagine that every time you breathe in, you are inhaling prana, the life energy of the universe, shining in gold. In this life force, you will find everything you need and desire: a healthy, muscular body, a self that loves itself in all circumstances, a hand that puts enough nutritious food on the table, a strong voice to say no to sabotaging your diet, a head that can say no to those who are trying to distract you from your ideas and goals. With each breath, you absorb these positive images and emotions.

See in front of you exactly what your life would be like if you got everything you wanted. Release your old self and start becoming your new self. Gradually restore your breathing to regular breathing. Feel the solid ground beneath you, open your eyes, and return to your everyday state of consciousness.

Meditation Exercise 2: Forgiving Yourself

Sit comfortably. Do not cross your feet because this will lock you away from the desired experience. Hold your hands together to connect your logical brain hemisphere with your instinct. Relax your muscles, close your eyes.

Imagine a staircase in front of you! Descend it, counting down from ten to one.

You reached and found a door at the bottom of the stairs. Open the door. There is a meadow in front of us. Let's see if it has grass, if so, if it has flowers, what color, whether there is a bush or tree, and describe what you see in the distance.

Find the path covered with white stones and start walking on it.

Feel the power of the Earth flowing through your soles, the breeze stroking your skin, the warmth of the sun radiating toward you. Feel the harmony of the elements and your state of well-being.

From the left side, you hear the rattle of the stream. Walk down to the shore. This water of life comes from the throne of God. Take it with your palms and drink three sips and notice how it tastes. If you want, you can wash yourself in it. Keep walking. Feel the power of the Earth flowing through your soles, the breeze stroking your skin, the warmth of the sun radiating toward you. Feel the harmony of the elements and your state of wellbeing. In the distance, you see an ancient tree with many branches. This is the Tree of Life. Take a leaf from it, chew it, and note its taste. You continue walking along the white gravel path. Feel the power of the Earth flowing through your soles, the breeze stroking your skin, the warmth of the sun radiating toward you. Feel the harmony of the elements and your state of wellbeing. You have arrived at the Lake of Conscience, no one in this lake sinks. Rest on the water and think that all the emotions and thoughts you no longer need (anger, fear, horror, hopelessness, pain, sorrow, anxiety, annoyance, self-blame, superiority, self-pity, and guilt) pass through your skin and you purify them by the magical power of water. And you see that the water around you is full of gray and black globules that are slowly recovering the turquoise-green color of the water. You think once again of all the emotions and thoughts you no longer need (anger, fear, horror, hopelessness, pain, sorrow, anxiety, annoyance, self-blame, superiority, self-pity, and guilt) and they pass through your skin and you purify them by the magical power of water.

You feel the power of the water, the power of the Earth, the breeze of your skin, the radiance of the sun warming you, the harmony of the elements, the feeling of well-being.

You ask your magical horse to come for you. You love your horse, you pamper it, and let it caress you too. You bounce on its back and head to God's Grad. In the air, you fly together, become one being. You have arrived. Ask your horse to wait.

You grow wings, and you fly toward the Trinity. You bow your head and apologize for all the sins you have committed against your body. You apologize for all the sins you have committed against your soul. You apologize for all the sins you committed against your spirit. You wait for the angels to give you the gifts that help you. If you can't see yourself receive one, it means you don't need one yet. If you did, open it and look inside. Give thanks that you could be here. Get back on your horse and fly back to the meadow. Find the white gravel path and head back down to the door to your stairs. Look at the grass in the meadow. Notice if there are any flowers. If so, describe the colors, any bush or tree, and whatever you see in the distance. Feel the power of the Earth flowing through your soles, the breeze stroking your skin, the warmth of the sun radiating toward you. Feel the harmony of the elements and your state of wellbeing. You arrive at the door, open it, and head up the stairs. Count from one to ten. You are back, move your fingers slowly, open your eyes.

Chapter 4.

Mindful Eating

Recognizing Physical Hunger

Step 1: Identify Starvation for the Situation

Five types of triggers instigate current overeating programming. All of them are explained below:

- *Social Incentives:* They eat to avoid feelings of inadequacy or to share a common experience, hoping that it connects them to the others. There is scientific evidence that we eat quite a lot when we eat in a social environment.

- *Sensual Trigger:* eat for an opportunity, eat donuts at work, advertise food for food on TV, or pass by the bakery. I didn't feel the need to nourish my body, but I had the opportunity to experience joy and suddenly felt hungry. In these cases, the desire to eat is an opportunity to experience the learned reaction, a pleasure to external triggers. We weren't hungry until we saw the visual food.

- *The motivation for thought:* Eating as a result of internal dialogue that condemns oneself. We offend ourselves, and ironically, succumbing to overeating usually reprimands us for lack of willpower.

- *Physiological trigger:* Eating in response to a physical effect (e.g., headache or other pain).
- *Emotional triggers:* Eating in response to boredom, stress, fatigue, tension, depression, anger, fear, and loneliness. These triggers are as simple as a lack of cognition in the body (I need a physical break) or as complex as suppressed emotions (I'm a member of a toxic family).

Step 2: Break the Obsession

My brain is crazy about food. I'm hungry and wired to make me feel obsessive about responding to food. This is my current wiring that uses food depending on different situational triggers.

Step 3: Name and Address Your Actual Needs

Depending on the situation, you have the option of how to respond effectively to the trigger.

- *Social Trigger:* To fulfill the desire to connect with others, I can try a few small bites and rave about the food. Even better, you can start an exciting conversation about something other than food. TCB Answer: This is not a pang of physical hunger. This is my desire to adapt to society.
- *Sensual Trigger:* Recognizing my usual reaction to the visual appeal of food. I admit I wasn't hungry before I saw the food. We must

admit that this is not physical hunger; it is an automated response to the unexpected.

TCB Answer: This is not a pang of physical hunger. This is my Pavlov's response to a highly charged stimulus. I want to enjoy the pleasure that food presents. If I eat this sweet, I will feel better.

- *Motivation:* Recognizing the usual reaction to negative thoughts, pain, and discomfort. Ending emotional stress is a normal human reaction. I have alternative and meaningful ways to deal with feelings of inadequacy.

  TCB Answer: This is not a pang of physical hunger. Eating is a way for me to calm down and how I weaken my painful thoughts. I have the tools or can get the help I need to deal with the painful dialogue inside.

- *Physiological triggers:* There are more effective tools (medication as needed) to deal with physical complaints.

  TCB Answer: This is not a pang of physical hunger. This is a learned response to physical illness.

- *Emotional triggers:* You can identify what triggers your emotional hunger and choose to act effectively.

- TCB Answer: This is not physical hunger. That is my standard coping mechanism and current wiring.

Step 4: Measure Progress

What about after performing steps 1-3? The scales in the Step 4-Measures of Progress and Experience of Success stages help you measure progress as you adopt individual characteristics. The more you practice, the easier it will be.

Is possible for you to respond to each signal in an appropriate manner? If the answer is no, what is your stress level? Need to reduce stress first? What are the wise decisions to meet your actual needs?

Take Time to Prepare a Healthy Meal

Home cooking has many advantages because it's a form of mindfulness. You personally choose high quality and nutritious ingredients. Keep in mind that grocery stores are based on cheap fats and cheap carbohydrates, not your nutritional value. You are controlling where your calories come from: they come from trans fats, additional sugars, well! They ensure that there are no flavor enhancers like MSG or other brain-disrupting substances

Think about it; you have to eat carefully. The only area that affects 95% of this possibility is the quality of the food you eat. If you don't know who cooks or exactly what ingredients they use, are they cheap trans-fat oils, lots of extra sodium, extra sugar? How can you manage yourself?

Sitting In Beauty

Establish a simple and beautiful environment, especially if you eat alone. Even if you're hungry, it can take a few minutes to reach an attractive setting. If you don't have the time, are in a hurry, and want to eat directly from the fridge, this is a big sign that you're usually absorbed in foods that are perceived as high levels of anxiety.

Remember to measure your progress. Can you set up the table without fear? If not, could you be wise to identify the cause of anxiety and address it?

Eating Experience

In a culture that emphasizes multitasking, eating is a secondary activity. We do not combine food with the nutrition of our bodies. Eating is what we do without attention while doing more meaningful work.

If you are dining with your family, invite them to participate in the careful process of eating. Trying to turn off as many distractions as you can during your meal is better than overeating during multitasking. Discuss your senses and taste of food. Slow food does not have to be extreme. Nevertheless, it is a good idea to remind the family that eating is not a race. Encourage the family to chew on every slice of food, examining the taste, texture, and odor in detail. Ask them about their feelings, thank them for collecting brownie points, and thank them for their blessings and share their meals with their families.

Remember to measure your progress: how do you feel in silence after a meal? Can you eliminate all distractions and eat quietly without fear? Is practicing this property easier to eat silently?

Enjoy Your Meal

Of course, the thin women have an internal dialogue of appreciation and appreciation and joy: "This is delicious. And it saturates. Shoveling food not only misses every bite of taste, but the entertainment center is in place. You'll need more food to meet gourmet merchants because you're not inspired by it.

Remember to measure your progress. How do you feel after allowing an internal dialogue about the pleasure of eating? Do you enjoy this conversation without fear? If the answer is no, what are the obstacles to achieving this trait?

Small Bites

If you overeat, you will burn more calories and experience the same amount of pleasure. We must recognize that we have made significant efforts in the past. The wise action is to eat some meals with a small spoon like a wheel while we learn to take smaller bites. However, once you measure progress in this area, it is essential to make the scoop larger. The reason is that if you take a small bite just because the spoon is low, the neural network won't be restored, and you are entirely dependent on the tool.

Don't forget to check for your progress. How does it feel like after eating the whole meal with just a few bites? How was your fear? Did you experience the fun with such a small morsel? Did you have to hit the kitchen and get a more oversized spoon? Or did you just start eating with your fingers?

Fork Down

Whatever your fork or tableware is placed in a bite, you are encouraged to eat wholeheartedly. We are ready to enjoy every bite, every subtlety, every spice, and every texture. Eating is foreplay, not a race. It's a sensual experience. Arashi defeats the purpose.

Remember to measure your progress: how do you feel after eating a complete meal and placing a fork in a bite? What is your fear level? Would you like to enjoy the delicacy of food?

Chew Slowly and Thoroughly

For many obsessive eaters, diet represents a solution for drug users. The faster you can move the shovel, the quicker you can get up. Unfortunately, this behavior leads to total calorie burn and shortens the sensation of pleasure. We try to raise our dopamine levels as soon as possible! We've been doing this for a long time, so biting slowly and slowly can be anxious.

Remember to measure your progress. How do you feel after biting slowly? What was your fear? Can you enjoy the slowdown without fear?

Breathing

After swallowing, breathing three times will reconnect with the body. If you prefer, it is a kind of palate wash. Readjust for the next bite sensual experience. This is also an opportunity to help us determine if we are full.

Remember to measure your progress. Do you breathe three times during one bite with one meal? Did you notice that your anxiety is growing? Did you enjoy your meal?

Experience Fullness

If you eat it carefully, you'll be full if you lose the taste! By contrast, they are looking for salt, ketchup, mayo, mustard, sugar, or barbecue sauces as overeaters. It's something you can regain a comfortable experience and "enjoy" your food. Additives are an attempt to nullify the intelligence that tells you that you have enough.

I've certainly heard the advice to wait 20 minutes for your brain to catch up with your ecstasy. But when we eat at piranha speed, we consume a lot of food. We don't know how to wait. Until then, everything was invisible. Besides, our brain isn't too slow! By paying attention to when food loses its initial appeal, we can instantly know when it is full.

Note that the beginning of this process feels strange. After all, we are used to consuming everything on the plate. For many of us, throwing away food is very difficult because our conditioning to eat everything on the plate is rooted. A useful tool is to visualize excess food as fat in your favorite body parts. Your taste will tell him that he is good enough, and all overconsumption turns into fat.

Also, understand that we are accustomed to stomach congestion and no food consumption. Initially, this is done mechanically, but if you repeat this a few times, you get the actual saturation. Besides, regaining confidence in the palate signal feels free, as you no longer need to experience the severity of a clogged sensation after a meal. The energy satisfaction after eating, rather than lethargy or immobility, regains your sense of freedom.

Remember to measure your progress. Can you say "it was great" and "I'm full" without having to stuff myself? Can you recognize the abundance?

Chapter 5.

Self Confidence and Self-love

Self-love is probably the best thing you can accomplish for yourself. Being infatuated with yourself furnishes you with fearlessness, self-esteem and it will by and large help you feel progressively positive. You may likewise find that it is simpler for you to experience passionate feelings for once you have figured out how to cherish yourself first. On the off chance that you can figure out how to adore yourself, you will be a lot more joyful and will figure out how to best deal with yourself paying little respect to the circumstance you are in.

Self-Confidence

Self-confidence is just the demonstration of putting a standard in oneself. Self-confidence as a person's trust in their very own capacities, limits, and decisions, or conviction that the individual in question can effectively confront everyday difficulties and requests. Believing in yourself is one of the most significant ethics to develop so as to make your mind powerful. Fearlessness likewise realizes more bliss. Regularly, when you are sure about your capacities you are more joyful because of your triumphs. When you are resting easy thinking about your abilities, the more stimulated and inspired you are to make a move and accomplish your objectives.

Meditation for Self-Confidence

Sit easily and close your eyes. Count from 1 to 5, concentrating on your breath as you breathe as it were of quiet and unwinding through your nose and breathe out totally through your mouth.

Experience yourself as progressively loose and quiet, prepared to extend your experience of certainty and prosperity right now.

Proceeding to concentrate on your breath, breathing one might say of quiet, unwinding, and breathing out totally.

In the event that you see any strain or snugness in your body, inhale into that piece of your body and as you breathe out experience yourself as progressively loose, quieter.

On the off chance that contemplations enter your psyche, just notice them, and as you breathe out to let them go, proceeding to concentrate on your breath, taking in a more profound feeling of quiet and unwinding and breathing out totally.

Keep on concentrating on our breath as you enable yourself to completely loosen up your psyche and body, feeling a feeling of certainty and reestablishment filling your being.

Experience yourself as loose, alert, and sure, completely upheld by the seat underneath you. Permitting harmony, satisfaction, and certainty to full your being at this present minute as you currently open yourself to extending your experience of harmony and happiness. And now as you experience yourself as completely present at this time, gradually and easily enable your eyes to open, feeling wide conscious, alert, better than anyone might have expected — completely present at this very moment.

Self-Love

Self-love is not just a condition of feeling better. It is a condition of gratefulness for oneself that develops from activities that help our physical, mental and profound development. Self-love is dynamic; it develops through activities that develop us. When we act in manners that grow self-love in us, we start to acknowledge much better our shortcomings just as our strengths. Self-love is imperative to living great. It impacts who you pick for a mate, the picture you anticipate at work, and how you adapt to the issues throughout your life.

There are such a significant number of methods for rehearsing self-love; it might be by taking a short outing, gifting yourself, beginning a diary or anything that may come as "riches" for you.

Meditation for Self-Love

To start with, make yourself comfortable. Lie on your back with a support under your knees and a collapsed cover behind your head, or sit easily, maybe on a reinforce or a couple collapsed covers. For extra help, do not hesitate to sit against a divider or in a seat.

In the event that you are resting, feel the association between the back of your body and the tangle. On the off chance that you are situated, protract up through your spine, widen through your collarbones, and let your hands lay on your thighs.

When you are settled, close your eyes or mollify your look and tune into your breath. Notice your breath, without attempting to transform it. What's more, see additionally on the off chance that you feel tense or loose, without attempting to change that either.

Breathe in through your nose and afterward breathe out through your mouth. Keep on taking profound, full breaths in through your nose and out through your mouth. As you inhale, become mindful of the condition of your body and the nature of your brain. Where is your body holding pressure? Do you feel shut off or shut down inwardly? Where is your brain? Is your brain calm or loaded up with fretfulness, antagonism, and uncertainty?

Give your breath a chance to turn out to be progressively smooth and easy and start to take in and out through your nose. Feel the progression of air moving into your lungs and after that pull out into the world. With each breathes out, envision you are discharging any negative considerations that might wait in your brain.

Keep on concentrating on your breath. On each breath in, think, "I am commendable," and on each breathe out, "I am sufficient." Let each breath in attract self-esteem and each breathe out discharge what is never again serving you. Take a couple of minutes to inhale and discuss this mantra inside. Notice how you feel as you express these words to yourself.

On the off chance that your mind meanders anytime, realize that it is all right. It is the idea of the brain to meander. Essentially take your consideration back to the breath. Notice how your musings travel in complete disorder, regardless of whether positive or negative, and just enable them to pass on by like mists gliding in the sky.

Presently imagine yourself remaining before a mirror, and investigate your very own eyes. What do you see? Agony and pity? Love and delight? Lack of bias?

Despite what shows up in the meditation, let yourself know: "I adore you," "You are lovely," and "You are deserving of bliss." Know that what you find in the mirror at this time might be not the same as what you see whenever you look.

Envision since you could inhale into your heart and imagine love spilling out of your hands and into your heart.

Allow this to love warm and saturate you from your heart focus, filling the remainder of your body.

Feel a feeling of solace and quiet going up through your chest into your neck and head, out into your shoulders, arms, and hands, and afterward down into your ribs, tummy, pelvis, legs, and feet.

Enable a vibe of warmth to fill you from head to toe. Inhale here and realize that affection is constantly accessible for you when you need it.

When you are prepared, take a couple of all the more profound, careful breaths and after that delicately open your eyes. Sit for a couple of minutes to recognize the one of a kind encounter you had during this meditation.

From the decrease of pressure, tension, sleep deprivation, and even agony, the advantages of contemplations to some degree continue deriding its naysayers. The more research directed, the more the past sentence bodes well. A huge number of research reports keep on demonstrating how contemplation impacts both psychological and physical prosperity. Meditation can conquer any hindrance among you and numerous common needs also: your rest shows signs of improvement, you can control your weight, your connections become progressively palatable and you can lessen physical torments that periodically travel in complete disorder. With regards to eating and dealing with our weight and our wellbeing, it is imperative to recognize the significance of the mind-body connection. Knowing this, allows you to make changes necessary to fit your current needs with the added ability to adjust in any new environment you encounter from here on and into the future.

Chapter 6.

Love Your Body, Heal Your

Soul

Happy people accept themselves and love each other no matter how their body looks, no matter how they feel. A perfect body is not inherently stronger or more inspiring than a body not considered being ideal by the "powers that be." You decide how you feel about your appearance.

For example, think of someone you know (or knew) who isn't necessarily all that sexy but who seems to care so much for herself that she feels amazing and behaves accordingly. These kinds of people seem to be very common. Interestingly, their beauty shines so brilliantly they seem appealing to others.

How do you feel about shaping your body? How about the state of your body? How do you feel healthy? Do you feel satisfied with your emotional and physical health?

What if your body does not suit media-based definition of the beautiful? Will that make you feel less attractive – or unattractive? Who sets the media unrealistic standards?

TV people usually don't look like they appear to be appearing on stage or in magazines and movies. That's why the Make-up artists' career exists. What they do in my mind is apply make-up depending on how the person looks to the audience and fans. Of course, when it comes to photo publishing no one is seen as they actually look. All pictures are touched up.

To whose standards are you sticking to? What if something changes for you? If you discover and describe your own beauty inside, then nothing changes how you feel about being you – nothing about your outer world.

When you love yourself, love yourself truly, no matter how old you grow to be your feelings about you, it won't change. The most fascinating piece of loving yourself is about living in a stable life. There are very few people who get to live there. Whoever remains young forever.

Ways to Love Your Body Now and Take the Road to Better Health

Drop the Tension Boom

Stress is among your mind and body's greatest enemies. No matter how intensively you work out if you keep high-stress levels your exercise and fitness routine will be sabotaged. Reducing stress is a key element that will show that you really care about your body. Yoga and meditation are two methods found to be effective by many people in countering stress. It doesn't really matter what you choose as a means of eliminating the stressors in your life as long as it's an activity that makes you happy and really eases the stressful demands on your mind and body.

Better Nourishment

You've heard this before several times but it still needs to be repeated. Your food choices have a lot to do with how you look, feel and react to your body. You have to learn how to make wise choices about the foods you consume daily. Fresh veggies and fruits will fuel your body. Throw out those over processed fast foods and prepare meal packages and discover the pleasure of eating healthy and show your body that you really care.

Weights Work Out

When it comes to loving your body, exercise is everything important. A full program of work out should involve both aerobic and anaerobic activities. You should include weights in your regular exercise routine, too. Working with weights not only will burn fat and help you get stronger but it will build bone strength which is a great bonus for your body.

Take Your Time

A little bit of self-pampering is not a luxury requirement. You must set aside an hour or two just to indulge yourself, at least once a week. For example, a relaxing, hot stone massage is a great way to relax. These tight muscles and painful joints are rejuvenated and you will find that you suddenly have a "new life lease." A relaxing spa day at a nearby lounge is always nice but in your own home, you can just as easily soak in a warm water pool. Set the mood with candles, flowers and aromatic oils and you'll quickly see the positive effect on your mind and body that this relaxing time has.

Go With the Flow

Perhaps the best way you can show your body how much you love it is by becoming attuned to the signals that it gives. When you start any workout or exercise routine you need to listen to those signals. Don't press for more than your body can supply. The pace on yourself as you develop strength and stamina. Do not compare yourself to others, because you have a unique body. Remember that getting in shape is a progressive marathon work and is not a 24-hour sprint. Take things up at a reasonable pace, and let the flow go. When you work for your body instead of against it, you will cross the finish line in top shape; and isn't that a real act of love?

Tips to Help You Love Your Body

1. Take Back The Power To Define Your Beauty

Not just take it back for the interpretations of culture/media, but also from people in your life around you who made judgmental remarks about your body. Such people couldn't see the body's uniqueness because they had absorbed the societal ideals themselves—and judged you and perhaps their own body by those expectations too. Take a moment to close your eyes now, and imagine taking back the power to describe your own body's beauty. Take it back from the cultural constructs and media-in your mind say "I'm not going to let you describe what my body will look like anymore." Think back to whoever made derogatory remarks about your body—a family member, a romantic partner or other children when you were young. Clear your own negative views about your body

2. Exercise For The Joy of Your Body's Movement

When you exercise to remove fat from your body and/or compensate for calories eaten—this can come from a place of fear and have the energy to try to control your body and fight it. Imagine exercising for the fun of moving your body and enjoying your body-a desire to be safe and have more strength. The clients I work with around this topic tend to be able to sustain an exercise routine; if they do so from a position of happiness and self-love instead of worrying and stressing for their weight.

3. When You Look at Yourself With Caring Eyes in The Mirror-Look

For many women looking in the mirror it turns into a self-judgment exercise. They zero in on all their perceived flaws in their body or face and what they believe is "false." Again, the criteria against which they judge themselves is this unrealistic ideal promoted in the media. I have a lot of clients who said they couldn't look in the mirror when they first started working with me, because all they saw were those perceived defects. What I suggested was to shift this by looking through loving eyes instead at themselves in a mirror. An example will be if you look into the mirror and see a wrinkle that you can normally judge – look with love and compassion at this wrinkle – and even see the beauty of that wrinkle. Set a strong intention to see yourself through the prism of love – interrupt your self-judgment and step towards being really self-loving. This will be something you need to practice before it becomes a habit – but the effort will be worth it because you'll start feeling very good about yourself.

4. Have Your Self-Esteem Referenced Internally

Have your self-esteem based on your inner qualities and not on your outward appearance. What qualities do you make? Is it your kindness, exceptional imagination, intellect, desire to have fun, wisdom, perceptiveness, desire to listen to people, or caring heart? Think of the people in your life that you love. You love them for who they are — the unique spirit they are — not because of what they look like. That's how they feel about you — they love you and all the unique qualities that make you up. Learn to respect yourself for your material — not for the physical manner in which you move.

5. Eliminate Comparison With Others

The strength of contrast and rivalry is harmful to you and the other person. Doing so is just another way to put yourself down and won't help you feel good but make you feel even worse. Instead, if you see someone who's attractive — instead of comparing yourself to that person or criticizing them — state instead — "She's attractive and so I am."

6. Take One of Your Usual Areas of Your Body and Take a Week to Enjoy This Part of You

Look at this part of your body for 15 minutes a day, and find things to love about it, better yet, do it all day. The more challenging this is, the more you have to do it! I once read in a paper about a woman who was doing this exercise and a stranger came up to her after a week of doing it and told her how beautiful this part of her body was! When we change our way of seeing ourselves—it completely transforms the way others see us. You want your original aim to do this exercise to be the change in your own self-love, not to influence how others see you. How you see you will always be what matters the most.

7. Decide That You Are Beautiful, and Do Beautiful

You get to determine whether or not you're cool. If you took back your power to define yourself, as I said above, then why don't you assert your own beauty! Take a day and repeat "I am Beautiful" to yourself, do things that make you feel something special-beautiful-wear-which you love and feel comfortable in. Drive like you are stunning. Look in the mirror and say "I'm beautiful." At first, this may feel awkward but continue to do so until you really start believing it. Celebrate who you are, and your unique and beautiful body. We need women who see and celebrate their own beauty — it helps other women who are stuck in their body's negativity to see that there's another happier path to take — the path of true self-love!

Chapter 7.
Parental Relationship Attachment style, Trauma, and Relationship with Food and Body

At the end of the day, the state of emotional eating is about seeking fulfillment and finding satisfaction. The problem is that the way in which you are choosing to do it won't give you what you truly need. Instead, it will harm your health and create further detachment between you and your true self. The connection that you are trying to create with emotional eating is the connection with your identity. You may see that as a way of looking for spiritual satisfaction using food. Indeed, with mindful eating and a self-loving attitude, food is a good source of pleasure and fulfillment. However, when the act of eating becomes a way for you to detach from your inner being, the trouble occurs. Meditation, self-reflection, and mindful eating can become a way for you to overcome emotional eating. This is because, with awareness and mindfulness, you will get to connect with your spiritual self. Your inner self remains unchanged and untouched by the difficulties of life, and holds a lot of knowledge and instinctive wisdom (Ross, 2016).

How Your Identity Affects Your Relationship with Food

To better understand the essence of your relationship with food, self-awareness is the right approach. To bring the matter closer to your understanding, you can frame the process of discovering the nature of your relationship with food through self-awareness as the process of connecting with your true identity.

Learning how to be in touch with your true identity means becoming able to access your inner strengths and instinctive wisdom. This way, the struggles of life won't overpower you, and you will be able to center yourself and regulate your feelings once challenges occur. This makes a lot of sense from a scientific viewpoint too, since your body and mind are constantly working to learn, grow, change, and self-preserve. What happened to you was that early trauma, in the broad sense of the word, taught you that hearing yourself out and trusting yourself was wrong or dangerous. For this reason, you were willing to disregard all of your knowledge and wonderful human qualities, and only look into what you perceive are lacks or flaws:

- You are overeating because you think that you can't handle your feelings, which isn't true;
- You are refusing to hear and acknowledge your most profound fears and insecurities that are a result of misinformation;
- You don't believe your own instincts because you deemed them to be a sign of weakness or selfishness. For that matter, you don't seek love, affection, care, and support either from yourself or from others;

How Early Attachment Affects Your Relationship with Food

From the moment you were born, you've associated food with love. Whether you were breastfed or not, the state of hunger was the most distressing experience for you at the time. Being hungry was an agonizing feeling, and receiving the food was a life-saving experience. There's nothing wrong with having a close connection with food. If you think about it, the lack of it, while you were a baby, caused your body to scream for attention. Can you imagine the level of agony you'd have to feel now, as an adult, to react the same way you did when you were a baby? Your initial relationship with food was that the lack of it meant pain and suffering, and getting it meant that you got attention, love, comfort, and care.

Insecure attachment with primary caregivers may have contributed to forming a dysfunctional relationship with food. As a result, food may become a way for you to replace what you feel is missing from your life, and obtain love instead of feeling empty and deprived.

Food could have also become a way for you to cope with boredom, as children are often offered snacks to calm down or to keep them from begging for attention from the overtired, overly busy caregiver.

One of the first steps to find your answer in relation to food is to discover what you are trying to compensate for with eating. You need to understand how food is serving as a replacement for truly satisfying your soul, and how to change emotional eating with a good habit that truly nourishes both your body and spirit. To examine your relationship with food, write down the following observations:

- The times of the day when you turn to food for comfort;
- The exact foods you crave at the time; and
- The way in which the foods you crave for make you feel.

Now, a simple way to solve the mystery is to take the food out of the equation, and simply connect the times of the day with what you've perceived you can gain with food. This simple exercise will help you discover the type of fulfillment you are looking for with food. This is what your inner self is craving, and because you lack either knowledge or skill to provide that, you are using food. You could be yearning for anything from joy and fun, to companionship and comfort.

How Your Body Image Affects Your Relationship with Food

Repeating the same process will help you discover the background of your body image issues and the way in which habitual eating fits into the equation. Here's how to explore the connection between body image and habitual eating:

• Write down the thoughts about your body;

• Write down the situations that trigger these thoughts;

• Write down the social situations that make you crave food; and

• Write down the feelings and thoughts that these situations cause you;

Are you noticing any patterns? Does your negative body image somehow reflect on what you think when you're with friends and family? Could these thoughts and feelings have something to do with social overeating? If so, what are your observations regarding this connection?

How to Create a Healthy Relationship with Food

To start building a healthy relationship with food, focus on the positive ways in which the food serves you and your body. Next, list all the positive ways you want to feel about your body. This will be the beginning of the shift in the way you look at food. Pay attention to that list, and write down how having the ideal body would make you feel.

- How would you feel about yourself if you looked the way you truly desire?
- What would change in your life?
- What would change for you at work?
- How would your relationships change?

The answers to these questions are your core needs in relation to your body image, and the good things that you will obtain from your transformed relationship with food. It could be a desire to be accepted, loved, cherished, adored, respected, that lies behind your emotional eating.

Now, look into the similarities behind using the food to distract yourself from the negative thoughts, and the core needs that will be fulfilled with an ideal body. Most likely, there are similar needs at both ends. There could also be differences.

Detach Self-esteem from Food and Weight

If you're used to associating the way you feel about yourself with your weight and the way you are eating, it is very likely to have a negative effect on both your eating habits and your self-esteem. As a result, you've never built up true self-esteem. You could have spent extensive amounts of time and money chasing after the ideal body, without realizing that the true problem lies in the lack of self-esteem. With food and dieting, you were looking for a way to feel better about yourself. Even reaching the desired weight and shape can't help self-esteem issues. You need to realize that your self-esteem is unconditional, and that it comes from your identity. It doesn't depend on either your achievements or the way you look. As long as you are thinking about self-esteem as something that is earned, or achieved, you will never truly have it. Only by looking at self-esteem as the inborn right to be honored and respected will you make progress.

You learned why your current relationship with food isn't beneficial, and why it came to be in the first place. The main shift that you want to make in order to recover from emotional eating is that of your consciousness. Instead of eating to avoid coping, you want to adopt a relationship with food that focuses on the nourishment of the mind and body.

Chapter 8.

Quick Way to Burn Fat

Have you ever found the safest and easiest way to efficiently burn fat and lose weight without working off your butt and getting starving to death? I have, and that's precisely why I've been looking for a long time for the safest and easiest way to burn fat quickly! Here's what I got.

A lot of people are struggling to lose weight, and there are many reasons behind this:

Some have a prolonged metabolism, and the fats in the foods they eat every day do not break down properly and store as body fat, which causes the excess fat and constant weight gains.

Some people lead a lifestyle that isn't very healthy because it has anything to do with the work they're in at the moment, which doesn't involve a lot of physical activity, or because they want to sit and snack on various kinds of foods that slow down the metabolism and get used to that kind of lifestyle before they even know it!

A significant explanation why some people put on weight is because of excessive sugar intake or simply because the amount of sugar in their blood is naturally high and allows them to gain weight, certain high levels of sugar and types of sugars cause diabetes, which is a significant factor and a significant issue behind unnecessary weight gain. There are many weight loss plans out there that tell you different simple ways to lose fat rapidly, and most of them don't work because they don't make things easier for any particular situation like diabetes, eating patterns, and so on. Drink Hot Tea. Although it's not clear how this occurs, researchers seem to have found that drinking 6 cups of cold water a day will increase the metabolism of bodies by about 50 calories a day. This is roughly the equivalent of 5 pounds a year being shredded. Now that does not sound like a lot, but it's a smart thing to do to lose those extra pounds, given that it's all done by drinking water only. Perhaps the safest way to drink filtered or distilled water rather than tap water.

Eat a little sun. It has been found that the chemical capsicum present in chili peppers lights up the metabolism. A report in the Food Science and Vitamin Logy Journal suggests adding chili peppers temporarily improves your metabolism and lets you consume more calories. Keep any handy to add to a plate or use red-pepper flakes to spice up a favorite sauce.

Breakfast is served every morning. Fact, breakfast is the main meal of the day. Eating a healthy breakfast ensures that after a long night's sleep, the metabolism goes. People who miss breakfast are almost fivefold more likely to become obese. When a good meal doesn't activate the metabolism in the morning, so the body has no real choice but to hold onto fat reserves.

Will that be tea or coffee. Yeah, caffeine is known to help improve metabolism. A cup of brewed tea has been demonstrated to enhance metabolism by 12%. Researchers assume that this boost is provided by the antioxidant called Catechins in the drink. Only note, when making your coffee, avoid artificial sweeteners or sugar and take it straight up. Evite the lattes in your nearest coffee shop too. They can taste sweet, but some may contain as much as 700 calories. That's about 1/3 of your average total caloric intake for the day.

Eat and Battle Fat Food. It has been shown that people who eat at least 25 grams of fiber a day burn fat by as much as 30%. This is almost equivalent to three daily servings of fruits and vegetables. You can also get whole-grain fiber from you. Just be aware that all these grains come from sprouted grains such as millet, spelled, and quinoa. Stop highly processed whole wheat loaves of bread, entire wheat kinds of pasta, and the like, which are considered "clean." When you eat these, all they do is turn to sugar in the digestive tract, resulting in more exceptional fat content.

In the fight against weight gain, the mind is a potent weapon. The trick is getting into an attitude that is going to drive you when things get tough. If you're able to persuade yourself that your target is achievable, you'll win half the battle. Most people give up on this because it is too difficult. If things get rough, or you want to throw them in the towel, take a step back and slow things down. Often the stuff of time is all in mind, and you'll see results if you can monitor your thoughts on this matter.

The Start Stage

Any journey, no matter how long and how complicated, begins with step number one. This may sound like a cliché, but it is genuinely absolute. You can go miles and miles down a path, and you'll finally get to your destination point if you keep on driving. Painting this image is only one thing you can keep in mind when you step on to try to change things for good.

Health matters a lot, so don't think you have to risk yourself to lose weight and burn fat, because that isn't real.

Ways for Constructive Thought to Rewire the Subconscious Mind

Whether or not we know our minds are divided into two parts—the conscious and the subconscious. The conscious mind governs our everyday activities and receives a surge of feelings and sensations that determine our daily attitudes and acts. In contrast, the subconscious mind is the protector of our deep, pre-existing set of beliefs that have been at the deepest level of our brains since early childhood. These unconscious, deep-seated beliefs play an enormous role in sending thoughts to the conscious mind, and more importantly, feelings.

Below are the top tips on how to rewire the subconscious mind and live consciously.

1. *Use the magic of I AM and gratitude.* Start thinking about the things you want as if you have them already but in very general terms. I want to joy, wellness, prosperity, and job achievement, for example. So I see myself happy and bright, look my best, have a beautiful day and say I'm delighted, I'm safe and fair—wow look at me! I AM stable and affluent—look at all the money around me! I AM in a career that feels like playing—watch me set my hours and work from home. Whatever works for you—speak it in the present tense, even if it has not yet

materialized. It will build a new system of confidence and emotion in the subconscious, which will enable you to take the required steps to make your imaginations very real. Never use phrases such as "I wish" or "I hope" as they mean that you cannot do what you want. I AM implies that you're willing to see that you can do what you want.

2. *Don't let anyone stop you from your childhood hardwiring or negative.* Most of us, in our most formative years, when the amygdala is exceptionally receptive to stimuli, received negative signals of fear and doubt. Typically those messages revolve around money. How many times have you heard stuff like "making money is hard" or "being rich is terrible?" You may have been shamed at your money behavior, or you may have had traumatic experiences involving money like an older sibling stealing from your piggybank, causing you to believe you don't deserve money subconsciously. May well-intentioned parents were always arguing over money, and you've been subjected to an angry dialog like "we can't afford that" or "how can we pay our bills this month?" Early experiences such as this have an impact on our adult behaviors about wealth, relationships, health, career, and happiness. It is up to us as adults people to understand that these are psychological issues that can be rectified with the right techniques of rewiring.

3. *Make daily positive affirmations.* Start the rewiring cycle with regular constructive affirmations that revolve around the places of your life that you want to change. I keep a list of statements that go something like this on my bathroom mirror: "I'm so thankful that

---

76

prosperity and success flow to me abundantly," "I'm healthy, wealthy and productive," "I'm thankful for my excellent health." Build a list of 10 positive affirmations and tape them into your bathroom mirror, front entrance, or anywhere you're likely to see them every day and speak them out loud! Your morale will be lifted, and the encouraging thoughts will continue to be part of the daily thought process.

4. *Create a list of what stops you from doing so.* You will sit down and figure out what your negative limiting values are, as they obstruct our growth and happiness. Take a notebook and enjoy a trip down memory lane. Try to find out what's hurting you about wealth, success, relationships, etc. Create a list of the things you might think of. When you've got a few things, you're generating positive affirmations that offset the negative effect on your life that early restricting belies had.

5. *Keep in the habit of expressing gratitude.* The surest fire way to get the juices flowing is to get into the habit of being thankful for everything. You eat the bagel for breakfast, the roof over your head, your career—everything you've already got. To be grateful for what you do traps you in the sense of abundance and flow that will contribute to the realization of more!

6. *One of the easiest ways to tap into your subconscious mind is to learn to meditate.* The internet is full of guided meditations you can buy and download or try to sit for 20 minutes in silence, focusing on a positive thought like gratitude. It will teach the brain to let ideas float, thereby making

it easier to release them. This, in effect, helps you learn to release unconsciously negative restricting thoughts that occur as a result of old programming.

7. *See it for yourself.* Training yourself to see yourself truly living the life you want is key to his ultimate realization. Visualize a significant amount in your bank account, see yourself participating in the job you like, or reasonably imagine your dream house. Do this in a peaceful place with your eyes closed and a big smile on your face for 3-5 minutes per day. This is the most effective method if you instill positive, happy feelings in the images—so smile big!

8. *Find happy people, with the same spirit.* The great advice I can give is to avoid negative people at all costs and start developing relationships with positive people who want the same things. Join social media account communities or find platforms that can reinforce your current belief system and reform efforts. Start gravitating at the workplace, the gym, and social situations toward more positive people. New relationships can also bring new opportunities.

9. *Find online videos that help your new mentality.* Help your reinforcement practice by watching videos about optimistic manifestation and brain reworking; you can easily find a wealth of videos in one of the popular search engines doing a simple search. Visual reinforcement is necessary, so don't miss this move, please.

Chapter 9.

Nourishing Your Love with

Food

Can a romance with food seem like something romantic and luscious, or does this seem like a head-on crash with fat gain? What type of relationship do you prefer to have food and eating? In your relationships, you will find two alternatives: you can select to maintain a relationship with an individual, or you could elect to become "unmarried" or "unattached." Even if somebody else chooses to maintain a relationship with you, you've got the choice to fall or runoff.

You do not have that choice with ingesting. You can't remove yourself from eating and food any more significant than you can discount breathing and air out of your life. Ever since your meals can't make the decisions about its connection with you, then you have to do the selection. You can't escape it. This query will remain valid: what type of relationship do you prefer to have food and eating? We all know people who inform us they hate to eat and find it a hassle to bother about it, preferring instead to have a pill if you were available. Besides, we know those who don't have a cooker and don't have any aim to cook or know-how. All of us have the freedom to choose what connection they'd love to have with meals. But because you're reading this publication, it's clear that people have something in common. Like people, you might love to consume and wish to relish food. We can opt to indulge ourselves at a passionate romance with food and enjoy our ideal weight.

You Can Eat Whatever You Want and Maintain Your Perfect Weight

At sixty years old we (the writers) discover that we're able to eat whatever we want and maintain our ideal weight. This capacity appears more real for us than other things. Let's repeat this, as it does capture the heart of our connection to meals. We could eat whatever we need — loving every little — and maintain our ideal weight. It's accurate to people, and it could also be accurate for you.

You Make it Happen

Luck isn't involved in getting a healthy, loving relationship with meals or other things. However, as anybody who's fallen in love understands, there's a particular magic to become in a relationship. There's a magic that focuses on your energy and utilizes your love to conquer any barrier powerfully. The energy or magic Which Makes this happen is on your decisions about What You Would like, or what inspires you, whatever you choose to think, and what you anticipate.

As we mentioned in the past phase, all these fundamental ingredients make other things to occur on your facts; to your ideal weight, this implies sensible food choices, exercise, and a lifestyle which generates the results that you desire. Another factor in your relationship with food is the intention and focus. "Intention" is the psychological idea about what you would like. "Care" is the energy or focus you put on what you're doing this will provide you with the outcome which you would like. As an instance, you plan to eat only enough to be full, rather than overstuffed. Your focus concentrates on chewing every bite mindfully, gradually and discovering if the body has had enough food. A healthy and loving relationship needs your goal and your focus to make the outcomes that you would like.

To nourish your pure romance with eating and food, let us look at the parallel into a healthy marriage or partnership. Bear with us, for you will find a few quite helpful tips which you can draw upon to your relationship with eating and food. On your relationship with meals, we'll primarily examine the components of choice, including homogamy, complementarity, and confidence.

These are the very same concepts or blockers included with a healthy, productive relationship or union. To begin with, we'd love to amuse the principle of "residential propinquity" that says what or who's nearest to you've got a much better opportunity for choice. Or simply put, you're more likely to meet and fall in love with someone close to you than with Somebody Who resides in another town, another country, or a different country. In the same way, locally grown foods are simpler to love. Locally grown foods are tastier and maintain increased nutrient energy compared to food that has been grown three million miles off and processed to endure a very long trip and also to get a long shelf life. Select what's near your foods which come from wherever you reside. Farmers' markets are among those matchmakers on your romance with food.

Homogamy

One filter in making a relationship entails homogamy, which signifies similar values and interests. You're more inclined to meet and fall in love with a person if you shout with individuals who share similar values and interests. For Example, if You like art galleries, you're more likely to discover a harmonious spouse if you enroll in an art course compared to if you shout with folks in a beach volleyball contest. The same goes for meals. If you'd like your ideal weight, you're more likely to attain that aim if you surround yourself with foods which encourage healthy fat, like fresh vegetables and fruits and whole grains, instead of with foods which aren't compatible with your ideal weight, like doughnuts, pizza, as well as fries.

Complementarity

That is the filter in which the differences between spouses improve the connection. The differences that you bring into the relationship are now able to serve one another's requirements and create the connection more reliable. In a venture, it may be the one spouse likes to perform lawn work and another dislikes it.

One likes to deal with the financing, pay off the bills, and also write the tests, while another spouse receives a stomachache while he or she sees the money fly from their checking account every month. The differences match the spouses because everyone serves the requirements of another. On your romance with meals, you can allow your meals to offer you protein fats and minerals which you can't manufacture yourself. And subsequently, you provide your meals with the body motions that burn off the calories and convert that the underlying food energy to some wanders through a beautiful park.

Your dinner provides you with a symphony of delicious snacks and delights. During your sleep nightly, the human body absorbs the nutrients through digestion to get healthy tissues, energy, and energy. The morning after, you simply take your own body to get a stroll or to a yoga class or offer it a workout which transfers the consumed nutrients to wherever they are now able to provide you with the ideal weight which you would like—seeing what high benefits food supplies can improve your relationship with meals. The next time that you're eating consider how much the meals will nourish the human body, along with your ideal weight.

Trust

All adoring relationships have to be based on confidence. Trust is not "hit or miss," nor does this happen acus on making it frequently occur so that it will become a habit. Keep in mind, and the aim is the psychological idea about what you would like. Care is your energy put on that which you do this will provide you with the results you desire. You ought to be in a position to be prepared in selecting foods that can provide you with the outcome you desire. Food shouldn't only satisfy appetite; it should also make the entire body weight you would like and psychological well-being. Your meals shouldn't irritate you. Foods that betray your wellness and ideal weight are the ones which supply calories with nourishment, including fast foods and other processed foods such as packed biscuits, doughnuts, and soft beverages.

Every day, you're making your confidence in your capacity to pick the foods that work to your wellbeing and ideal weight, not contrary to your wellness and perfect weight reduction. By being aware of the internal cues for hunger and fullness, then you find what's "right" for you, which allows you to provide these meals that your confidence. You must also have the ability to trust that the food you're eating to provide the nutrients which meet your body's requirements along with your appetite. By remaining faithful to a connection with meals, you do not just develop the capability to decide on the foods that provide what you want with joy, but also you create a palate that enjoys these wholesome foods.

These pleasing foods are very fresh, critical, and teeming with nourishment and health and fantastic taste. If your food isn't tasty and gratifying, pick again. As time passes, you find you could trust the connection you've made to maintain your lifestyle and eating fashion which allows you to eat anything you need and maintain your ideal weight.

Chapter 10.

Taking Care of Yourself

We've got all watched young kids and how they consume their world: eyes wide open, tasting, touching, smelling, listening, and all with pleasure, complete impulse, along with energy and movement. We welcome you to approach this thing using the same childlike curiosity. You might select and choose what appeals to you personally and your ideal weight, what calms your bodily appetite, and that which motivates and inspire you.

Starving for Wholesome Foods – Heal "Eativity"

Our bodies are composed of billions of cells, and these cells will be the cornerstone of each use of the human body: vision, fertility, breathing and mind functions, immunity and skincare, motion, and nourishment, among the tens of tens of thousands of purposes. The food that we consume is the sole sustenance readily available for our bodies to make and replace those cells. The energy of each one of these cells depends on the calibre of food that we consume. If we consume foods that are healthy and nourishing, then the cells will likely be persuasive and vital. If we consume nutrient-poor foods, junk foods, processed foods, foods high in sodium, sugar, and fats that are bad, or highly processed foods, your cells will likely be feeble and will fight to do their roles.

Highly processed foods (that can be nutrient-poor) are usually quite high in carbs. A poorly ventilated body wants nutrition, and if this craving only contributes to more junk foods, then there are much too many calories eaten without a nutritional supplement gratification. Bad health and surplus weight may accompany. It may be a continuous cycle before it's broken with healthful foods. That's precisely why 65 percent of all Americans are obese. Their undernourished bodies have been overfed with inadequate food selections. As soon as we nourish our bodies with all healthy foods, we feel much better, have more energy, and therefore are more physically active; along with healthful weight is the outcome.

Everything we consume should bring about our wellness and be downright delicious. Our customers hear us say that this all of the time. It may be confusing to decipher what foods are healthy and contribute to your wellness. There's a single straightforward statement to keep in your mind that can clarify each of the vexing nourishment input yelling at us in TV, magazines, novels, and supermarket shelves. The healthiest meals, the foods that nourish our bodies the very best, are nearest to nature. These meals are all fresh, alive with brilliant colors, aromas, and flavors.

They are processed; they aren't canned, not suspended, not maintained, not artificially flavored, although not so colored with coloring agents, not hydrogenated not genetically engineered, but not sprayed with pesticides, although not only elevated with agrichemicals, not heat treated, although not homogenized. They're nearest to the character. At this time, you may be thinking there is not much left to consume after reading this. Perhaps you simply took a mental stroll through your kitchen. Perhaps you're frowning and standing facing your favorite crackers, biscuits, cake mixes, frozen TV dinners, ice cream, hot dogs, and pizza. The point is there are many highly processed foods accessible it is frequently a struggle to find the wholesome foods. However, you have to see them. You are interested in being hungry for healthy foods since they encourage your excellent wellness and ideal weight.

It Starts With a Couple of Tiny Tastes

Take the following psychological walk through your kitchen. Can you find any new fruits, fresh veggies, brown rice, legumes, almonds, or even sunflower seeds? If this is so, you have some healthful foods in your cabinet. All we're encouraging you to have to do is have a few little tastes, to look at making a couple of straightforward shifts toward sensible meals customs.

We'd like to introduce one to this Behavioral Nutrition Continuum. It's a beneficial instrument that you utilize in creating shifts in foods and lifestyle options. The initial step is locating your starting location on the nourishment continuum. However, the left of the continuum are people whose diets consist mainly of fatty, nutrient-poor foods: high in salt, fat, and sugar highly processed; along with nonorganic.

They're the product of their fast-food motion, and additionally, they aren't conscious of their environment surrounding food the people who, what, when, where, why, and how. Moving toward the ideal end of this continuum, we locate people whose diets consist mainly of whole foods, like grains, legumes, and fresh vegetables and fruits, and fewer animal meals.

These meals have been nutrient-dense, fresh, and alive with vivid colors, aromas, and flavors and are near to nature. Have you any idea where you're on this continuum? Where are your loved one's members and friends with this continuum? When you find individuals, who have bodies such as the one you need, odds are they are nearer to the ideal end of the continuum. Just know about your place on the continuum currently. It isn't important where you are. The most important thing is the direction you're moving.

Where you are will shift with time since you use only your awareness and start with a couple little and comfortable shifts. Through time, we've found that it's of extreme value to maneuver at your comfortable speed. It permits your taste buds and palate lots of time to lose the salty-sweet, creamy flavors that have mastered your plate for possibly many decades, and also to start savoring the refreshing tastes of healthful foods. So, begin where you're about the Behavioral Nutrition Continuum. And begin with a couple of tiny tastes of healthy foods, which direct you into the direction that you need to go.

How to Know What You're Eating

Another helpful tool is learning how to decode the Nutrition Facts and Ingredients tags which are on all prepared, canned and frozen foods. Both tags are significant but also for different reasons. The Nutrition Facts label defines amount, along with the Ingredients tag defines quality. Walk into your kitchen and choose a Nutrition Facts label out of some other packed merchandise. The tag includes information concerning the relative levels of different nutrients at the specified meals. As you can see, serving size and servings per container will be said first. The number of calories a serving and calories in fat have been recorded next.

The part immediately after lists in g the entire fat, saturated fat, cholesterol, total carbohydrate, dietary fibres, sodium, sugar, and protein inside every serving. Even the micronutrients, the minerals and vitamins, are recorded next. Additionally, the daily percentage value (a pair of regular nutrient consumption values created from the FDA) is calculated upon the tag and is founded on a 2,000-calorie nutritional supplement plan. It signifies is that if you are eating 2,000 calories each day, the daily percentage value said besides a nutritional supplement recorded on the item lets you know what proportion of your everyday requirements for that nutrient have been fulfilled by that item. You should develop the habit of studying all of the food labels on your kitchen and in the grocery shop.

When analyzing labels, ensure you relate the number of calories into the dosage size. Frequently the stated dose size is minimal, with a corresponding low-carb advertisement. For instance, a candy bar can promote only 50 calories a serving; however, that the serving size is merely a little portion of it, but maybe not the whole pub. But if you've got them on your kitchen (if not look next time you're in the grocery store), then pick the Nutrition Facts labels of 2 similar items like crackers or biscuits.

Compare the types of full fat, saturated fat, cholesterol, and glucose. Notice when a commodity advertises it is low carb, it's frequently full of sugar. When it promotes jelqing, it's frequently full of fat. Now examine the Ingredients tag that lists the real contents of an item. Incidentally, to see this tag, you may need to put on eyeglasses.

The Ingredients tag is notorious for being not able to see, because of instant print, absence of contrast between background and letters, or being published onto the fold of this wrap. The Nutrition Facts label can say the entire fat is 4%; however, the Ingredients tag will specify that oil or fat the food comprises (olive oil, cottonseed oil, partially hydrogenated jojoba oil, etc.)

Another instance where the Ingredients tag clarifies quality entails content. If the Nutrition Facts label lists total carbohydrates as 42 g, an individual can peek in the Ingredients tag and determine if the carbohydrate comes from white bread or some more health-promoting grain like bulgur, brown rice, or amaranth. The Ingredients tag also alerts the customer around food additives and animal products, a lot of which can be of concern.

A food additive is a substance added to foods through its processing to maintain it or change its color, texture, taste, or worth. Flavoring agents compose the largest single category of additives and contain additives, spices, essential oils, and natural and artificial flavors. Additives that change feel include emulsifiers like lecithin, stabilizers, and thickeners like guar gum, Xanthium gum, and carrageenan.

The additives used to maintain food are mostly chemical parasitic agents such as benzoates, propionates, and sorbates. Antioxidants are added to foods to prevent oils and fats from becoming rancid and to reduce discoloration of roasted or smoked meats. Antioxidants like tocopherols, vitamin E, vitamin retinoid, vitamin A, ascorbic acid, and vitamin C help retard spoilage. There's controversy regarding the security of several additives, so prepare yourself.

Water, Water Everywhere

Drink a massive glass of plain water first thing in the afternoon. It makes it possible to keep hydrated and flushes toxins out and also the ordinary wastes happening from metabolism. During the remainder of your daily life, drink plain water whenever you're thirsty. By eating a lot of vegetables and fruits that you can get roughly 40% of the water that you need from the food. Does water suppress your desire? No! Though being well hydrated keeps excellent metabolism, even drinking a fantastic deal of water doesn't lessen the quantity you consume. Water drains from the stomach promptly.

To feel complete with less, consume foods, which have high water content, like fruits, vegetables, and soups that are clear since they empty slower in the gut compared to plain water.

Breathe in, Breathe Out

Breathing is very literally "inspiration." Deep breathing generates optimal oxygenated blood and guarantees a very effective utilization of body and mind: from believing to optimal physical action. Sit through the nose four times, hold for 2 points, and breathe eight points. Concentrate on the sound of your breathing. Notice how pressure dissolves, the pressure is released, recovery is eased, overall well-being is apparent, and ideal weight is encouraged. Repeat this breathing exercise at least two times daily, but no longer than four breaths at every clinic at first.

Chapter 11.

Portion Control Hypnosis

Portion control tends to be a skill that many people struggle with. Knowing how to eat just enough to help yourself feel satisfied and full, without overeating, can be challenging. This is made even more challenging if you tend to be a stress eater or someone who goes long periods of time without eating and then binge eats. Portion control is an incredibly important element of weight loss as it provides you with the opportunity to get the proper nutrients into your body without overdoing it. As well, if you choose to satisfy one of your cravings or enjoy something more indulgent, portion control enables you to do so without going overboard.

The truth is: most people can eat anything in moderation and not suffer any unwanted consequences from eating that food. For example, if you want to enjoy a piece of brownie with your coffee at the café because you have been craving a brownie, there is typically nothing wrong with doing that. The key is to make sure that you enjoy the brownie, and then you *stop*. Rather than enjoying that brownie, then eating another piece, then going home and having even more junk food, enjoy that one brownie and then let yourself get back on track with healthy eating. When you can mindfully engage in portion control this way, you can eat just about anything you want without having any problems.

In fact, many famous diets rely more on portion control than anything else because they recognize that portion control is more effective than restricting what people can and cannot eat. The key with portion control is knowing how to actually feel satisfied by your controlled portions, and knowing how to stay committed to them. For many people, this can be challenging. You may feel so happy about eating your brownie or your piece of cake that you want more immediately after. Of course, if you immediately indulge, then you are not effectively engaging in portion control. However, if you instead let yourself enjoy that piece as much as you possibly can and then go back to eating healthy immediately after, then there was no big deal.

Rather than relying solely on portion control as a tool, it is important that you rewire your mind around why you struggle with portion control as it is. Getting to the root cause of your own struggles with portion control, healing your overeating challenges, and rewiring your mind around portion control can be incredibly helpful in allowing you to get what you need out of your diet. This way, rather than dealing with that internal conflict around, "I should stop," you stop naturally because your mind is already wired to stop naturally. As you might suspect, this can be done with subconscious work and hypnosis. However, there are also some conscious-level changes that you should make and things you should become mindful of so that you can navigate portion control both with your conscious mind and your new subconscious habits. This way, you are more likely to be successful with portion control in general.

Why Do People Overeat?

There are many different reasons why people overeat, although emotions and poor eating habits tend to be the most common ones that people experience. Another reason behind overeating can actually be an eating disorder, which may be caused by underlying conditions such as depression or anxiety, genetics, or other illnesses. If you do have an issue with compulsive overeating and struggle to keep it under control, talking to your doctor is an important way of ruling out possible illness factors that could be contributing to your problems.

When it comes to emotions, everything from stress and anxiety to sadness or discomfort can trigger someone to want to overeat. Believe it or not, the majority of our serotonin and other hormones are produced in the gut. Because of this, when you are feeling stressed out, anxious, sad, or otherwise uncomfortable, you might find yourself craving food. Most people will find themselves craving something specific, such as sweet or salty foods. Other people may find that they are willing to eat whatever is nearby in order to receive that "release" from having something yummy to eat. While overeating due to emotional causes every once in a while, may not necessarily be a bad thing, it is easy for this behavior to turn into a habit. Many people find themselves struggling with overeating due to emotional causes, although stress and sadness tend to be the leading causes of overeating.

Learning how to fix your eating habits by eating more consistently and eating healthier portions at proper meal times is an important way to take care of yourself. Eating regular meals will prevent you from binge eating later on due to being excessively hungry.

Getting to the Root Cause of Your Binge Eating

Understanding your own binge eating habits is important, as this allows you to develop a conscious awareness and a sense of mindfulness around why you are binge eating in the first place. When you are able to understand why you binge eat, resolving the root cause of your binge eating becomes easier because you know what to look for and what to be aware of.

Getting to the root cause of your own binge eating can be done by reflecting on your own binge eating cycles and, if necessary, tracking your binge eating cycles so that you can start to identify any possible patterns that exist around your binge eating behaviors. You can easily do this by keeping a food diary, which is a journal where you log everything you have eaten in a day. Make sure that you write down the time that you ate, what you ate, and how much you ate. Track everything, including little snacks in between. They may not seem significant, but you might be surprised to see how they add up and what comes of those snacks. Often, people find that they are unaware of how problematic their snacking has actually become until they begin to track it.

As you begin looking for the root cause of your binge eating, you might find that there are actually a few root causes. Often, however, most binge eating patterns can be traced back to one "major" root problem that seems to create more problems than the rest. For example, you might find that you have poor eating habits and often find yourself craving low-quality food, but you might realize that this largely stems from you being an emotional eater. Or, you might find that you are an emotional eater because you have poor eating problems and so you realize that, during a moment of stress, eating is one thing you can take care of while everything else might seem out of your control.

It is important that you take the time to identify every single root cause of your binge eating and not just the one that stands out the most. If you are going to have the biggest impact on changing your binge eating patterns, you are going to need to know everything that contributes to your binge eating so that you can be mindful of what might be triggering this behavior. If you do not focus on and heal *all* of your root causes for binge eating, you might find yourself binge eating out of habit and justifying it by different root causes every single time. The more thorough you can be with healing this, the more effective you will be, too.

With that being said, you may find it to be particularly overwhelming to attempt to actually resolve all of your root causes at once, especially if you have a few. If it does feel overwhelming, you can focus instead on just dealing with the biggest one and then healing one root cause at a time. This way, you can make a significant impact on healing your binge eating problems, but you are still able to remain mindful and aware of your other binge eating triggers.

Learning to Avoid Temptations and Triggers

Once you have a clear understanding of what your binge eating cycles and patterns are like, you can start implementing change to help you avoid temptations and triggers. There are many ways that you can reasonably avoid temptations and triggers when it comes to eliminating binge eating; however, you are going to need to focus just as much on your mindset as you do on your behaviors if you want to truly change. This is where meditation is going to help you really begin to start engaging in proper portion control so that you are no longer at risk of binge eating anymore. With meditation and hypnosis, you can begin to resolve the deep subconscious reasons behind your binge eating behaviors so that you have an easier time actually adhering to your changes. The more you engage in this deep healing, the easier it is going to be for you to make conscious and mindful changes in your eating habits, too.

As you use meditation and hypnosis to help you stop binge eating, you also need to focus on actually intentionally avoiding temptations and triggers. There are many practical ways that you can mindfully eliminate these temptations and triggers from your life. For example, you might intentionally stop buying the types of foods that you regularly binge eat so that the temptation no longer exists to begin with. You might also make sure that you eat on a consistent schedule so that you are no longer fasting to the point of being so hungry that you cannot stop yourself. If that is hard for you, picking up habits like meal prepping is a great opportunity for you to prevent yourself from waiting too long between meals and then binge eating as a way to make up for missing out on foods.

Another important way to start overcoming binge eating is to recognize that emotions can be a major trigger. In recognizing that, you can choose to identify and enlist new coping methods to help you navigate emotions in a healthier way that does not include binge eating. This way, you are more likely to manage your emotions with proper emotional management tools, rather than trying to numb yourself with the satisfaction that you get from snacking on junk foods.

Chapter 12.

Overcoming Mental Blocks

What beliefs are holding onto your weight?

- ➤ I am inferior
- ➤ I am lacking
- ➤ I am inconsequential so I have to make myself big to be seen
- ➤ Losing weight is too difficult
- ➤ I will fail and put the weight all back on again
- ➤ I must be so awful and bad not to be able to control my eating
- ➤ I want to punish myself
- ➤ It is too hard to start dieting
- ➤ My weight is ancestral, and I can't change that
- ➤ My weight is genetic, and I can't change that
- ➤ I am not good enough/I am not enough
- ➤ I self-sabotage myself
- ➤ I am worthless
- ➤ I loathe myself
- ➤ Healing negative beliefs

This means that you block your weight loss as you feel that the task is too daunting, and you will fail.

A block is something that stops you moving forward and the biggest one of these is fear. The other one is being safe. If your subconscious feels that it is not safe it will not let you do it. So, if your subconscious feels that losing weight is not safe, you will not lose weight!

Also, if you think you are worthless or you feel you do not deserve, this will cause you to self-sabotage.

What is Self-Sabotage?

The term, self-sabotage, describes our often-unconscious ability to stop ourselves being, doing or having; being the person we want to be, doing what we want to experience or achieve or having our goals and desires become reality.

Most of the time we are totally unaware that we are self-sabotaging as it happens on a subconscious level. However, sometimes we are aware of that little voice in the back of our head that says, "you can't learn a language" or "don't be a fool you can't lose weight."

Our subconscious mind is a powerful tool and always thinks that it is acting in our best interest. Stopping us stepping into new territory, discouraging us from taking risks ensures that we don't get hurt, we are not humiliated, and we don't fail — that is why so many projects never get off the ground. Rather than playing to win, self-sabotage plays to avoid defeat.

The purpose of this aspect of the subconscious is self-protection and survival. It can even negatively affect your health if it thinks that this will protect you from greater risk. Layers of excess weight have long been recognized as protection and very often the subconscious will use weight gain to protect you from perceived dangers you might be exposed to as a slimmer person. For example, where someone has been abused as a child, the subconscious may add weight to make them unattractive (it thinks) so that the abuse is never repeated.

So, people may talk about self-sabotage in regard to their weight because they eat emotionally and put on weight. However, sometimes self-sabotage will affect your hormones and/or organs, causing weight gain in people who eat only a modest amount. Sometimes people can lose weight but always put it back on just another method of self-sabotage. Once the perceived need to protect through self-sabotage has been healed and released, our illnesses and weight may disappear.

Emotional and Comfort Eating

When you read magazine articles they always talk about emotional eating and weight gain. Some people do eat for emotional reasons and boredom. Some people do overeat and there are explanations for this. You need to identify your emotional eating triggers and use a technique such as EFTTM to eliminate them. However, if you want to eat try to wait for 10 minutes breathing deeply and you should find that after that the need to eat has gone.

However, I know a lot of slim people who overeat and drink too much. They overeat for emotional reasons as well — slim people aren't perfect or without their own problems.

Removing the Self-Sabotage

When I was spending a huge amount of money with therapists and nothing worked, I did mention that I might be self-sabotaging myself. Most of them threw their hands up in horror and told me it was just an excuse to overeat (here we go again, I thought).

I read a lot about the Emotional Freedom Technique (EFTTM) and in the very first paragraph, I read it mentioned self-sabotage. This was quite amazing. However, my self-sabotage was so deeply ingrained that for a long time EFTTM just made everything worse, as my subconscious tried to hold onto its control of me.

I, therefore, had to dig much deeper by clearing the attachments, past lives, and karma and then I could use EFTTM and my other techniques to change my subconscious perception and its belief system that "I did not deserve."

Psychological Reversal

I thought I wanted to lose weight, but I actually didn't and my subconscious was stopping me. You need to find out all the reasons why and release and heal them one by one. For this, you use the EFTTM psychological reversal techniques.

How are you self-sabotaging because my experience would lead me to believe that you are?

Habit of Self-Sabotage

I had a spiritual reading session and was told that the self-punishment had been healed but that I still had the 'habit' and that needed to be healed and not recreated. I feel it is very important to include it in this book, as it would have never occurred to me that I still had the habit and was capable of recreating the habit at any time. Our body and subconscious sabotage us so much that it becomes automatic and then a habit. So even when the original stimuli are healed the habit remains. So, remember to test to see whether there is a habit and then heal accordingly (normally the same way you healed the original pattern). Make sure you don't recreate the habit by repeating affirmations and if you feel yourself slipping back into 'deserving the pattern' immediately cancel this feeling and ensure that you keep healing it.

What is the Secondary Gain?

Believe it or not, every illness and problem can have a significant benefit for the person who is experiencing it. Professionals use the term 'secondary gain' for this well-known phenomenon and you will start to recognize this behavior in people that you know. In some cases, the benefits of having the problem are so great they outweigh the suffering the problem is causing.

This problem is created by the subconscious, totally unbeknown to the person. Often this person is pushing themselves too hard and the unconscious mind will come up with a way to deal with what is going on in that person's life so an illness or a problem is created that is not under their control.

A good question to ask yourself is "what are the benefits to you that this illness or the problem bring and why are you keeping it around?" So, what are the benefits of you holding onto the excess weight? Analyze this question very carefully and dig until you get to the bottom of it.

> ➤ Watch your thoughts, for they become your words.
> ➤ Watch your words, for they become your actions.
> ➤ Watch your actions, for they become your habits.

- ➢ Watch your habits, for they become your character.
- ➢ Watch your character, for it becomes your destiny.
- ➢ Your subconscious believes everything it hears!

Remember that your subconscious listens to what is said to you by other people or yourself and it takes everything it hears literally. It cannot differentiate between a joke and reality, so never put yourself down, even as a joke. So, if you keep telling yourself that you are FAT your subconscious will make you fat and keep you that way. Your fat cells will think — I am fat, so I better keep my cells nicely plumped up and not lose them. Yes, this is really true!

I know it sounds amusing, but this is what happens in real life and the wonderful poem displayed at the top of the page becomes your reality — and what you believe becomes your truth.

Most people who are overweight are normally very critical and always speak negatively about themselves. They normally suffer from low self-worth and low self-esteem. The result is that, by doing this, they are perpetuating the problem. When you are speaking negatively to yourself, ask yourself if you would speak to a friend like that. The answer most probably will be that you wouldn't, so why on earth are you speaking like that to yourself? Stop it now!

It is almost impossible for your body to change when you keep sending it negative messages. As long as you say, "I am FAT," you give your body more instruction and energy to BE FAT.

Change 'I am fat' to 'I am getting slimmer every day'

Change 'I never lose weight' to 'It gets easier every day to lose weight'

Changing Beliefs

People ask how they can change their beliefs and luckily these days there is a variety of techniques and therapies to help do this, but you also have to be careful not to fall back into any bad habits.

This relates to all areas in your life and not just to weight, so let me tell you a couple of stories:

I love Sunday nights as this is my pamper night where I have a long bath, face mask and do my nails. Some of my friends hate Sunday night because they have to go back to work on Monday and they don't like their jobs. I have changed my perception of Sunday night so that I enjoy it, unlike my friends who dread it.